I Am a Sea Horse

The Life of a Dwarf Sea Horse

by Trisha Speed Shaskan illustrated by Todd Ouren

Special thanks to our advisers for their expertise:

Jonelle Verdugo, Associate Curator of Fish and Invertebrates
Monterey Bay Aquarium, Monterey, California

Terry Flaherty, Ph.D., Professor of English
Minnesota State University, Mankato

I Live in the Ocean

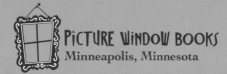

PiCTURE WiNDOW BOOKS
Minneapolis, Minnesota

Editor: Shelly Lyons
Designer: Lori Bye
Page Production: Melissa Kes
Art Director: Nathan Gassman
Associate Managing Editor: Christianne Jones
The illustrations in this book were prepared digitally.

Picture Window Books
151 Good Counsel Drive
P.O. Box 669
Mankato, MN 56002-0669
877-845-8392
www.picturewindowbooks.com

Printed in the United States of America.

 All books published by Picture Window Books
are manufactured with paper containing at
least 10 percent post-consumer waste.

Library of Congress Cataloging-in-Publication Data
Shaskan, Trisha Speed, 1973-
I am a sea horse : the life of a dwarf sea horse / by Trisha
Speed Shaskan ; illustrated by Todd Ouren.
p. cm. — (I live in the ocean)
Includes index.
ISBN 978-1-4048-4728-6 (library binding)
1. Sea horses—Juvenile literature. I. Ouren, Todd, ill. II. Title.
QL638.S9S43 2008
597'.6798—dc22   2008006345

I have a horse's head, and I'm wearing a crown. I have a long snout. My fins look like tiny butterfly wings. My long tail can curl around a plant stem. I am called a dwarf sea horse, but I am actually a fish.

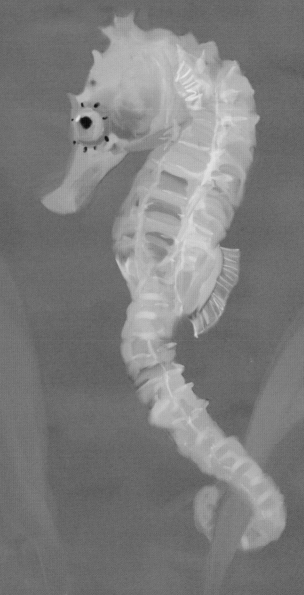

A sea horse doesn't have scales. Instead, it has a thin layer of skin. The skin is stretched over rows of bony plates. The plates look like rings around the sea horse's body.

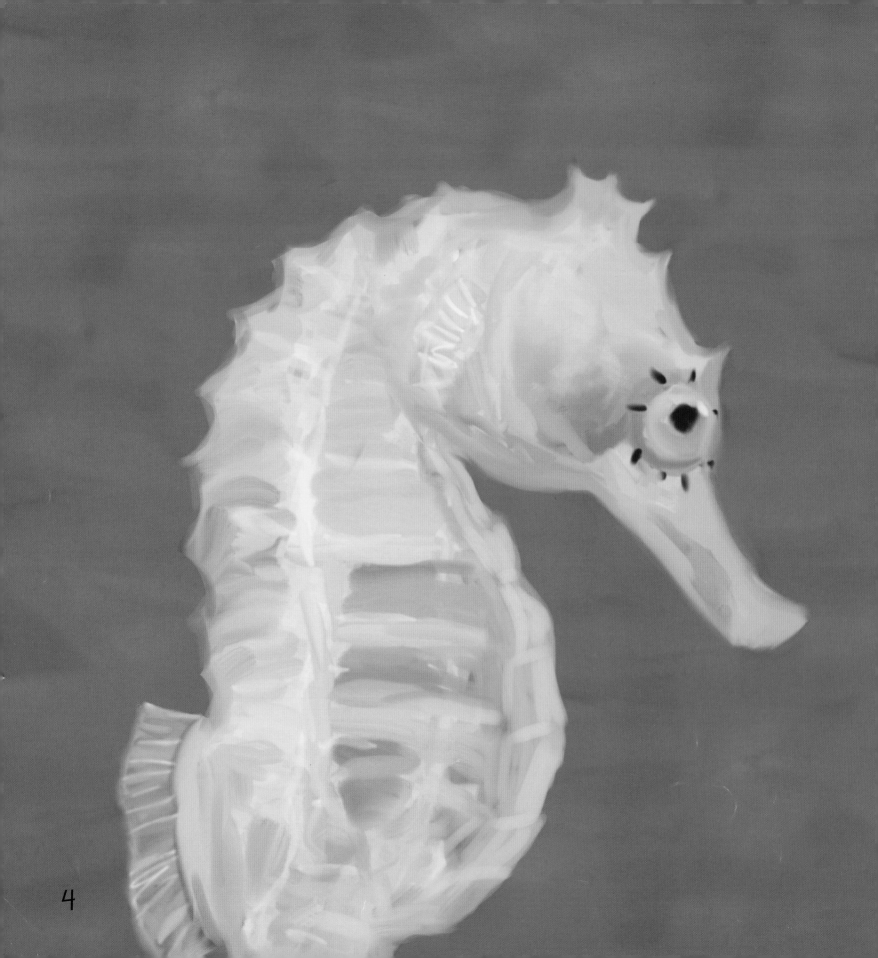

4

I wouldn't be here if not for my parents. When their eyes met, their bodies flashed bright yellow. Soon they were swimming side by side.

A sea horse can move each of its eyes in different directions. This helps a sea horse find food and avoid being eaten by other fish.

My mother and father spent days getting to know each other. They swam and danced through the water, changing colors and holding onto each other's tail. They became partners.

A sea horse will most likely have only one partner during its entire life.

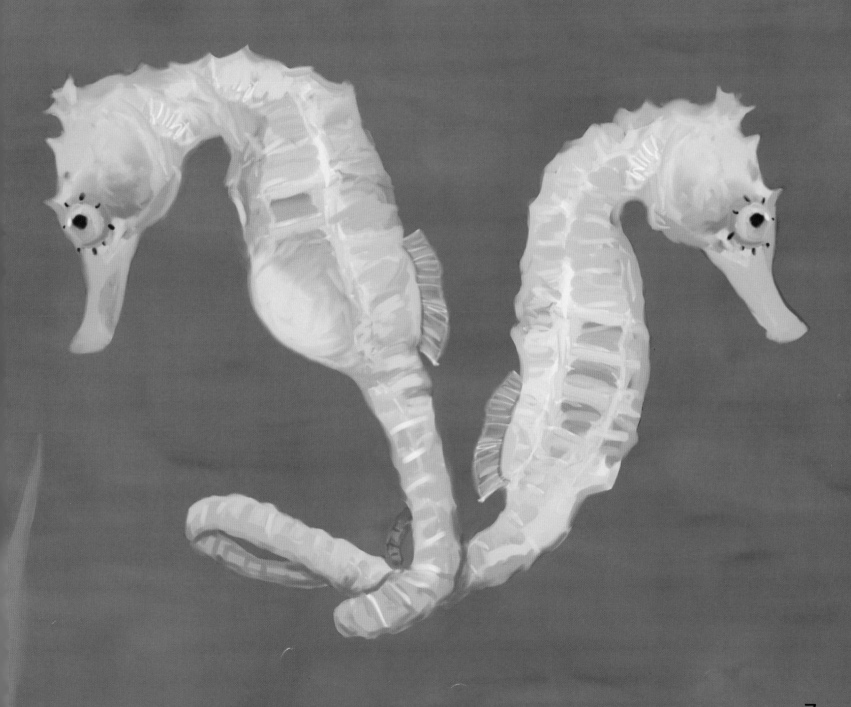

Soon, my mother dropped her eggs into my father's brood pouch. He carried the eggs. Each day that my father held the eggs, my mother would visit. The two of them danced and held tails. And all the while, I grew inside of my father's pouch, alongside my brothers and sisters.

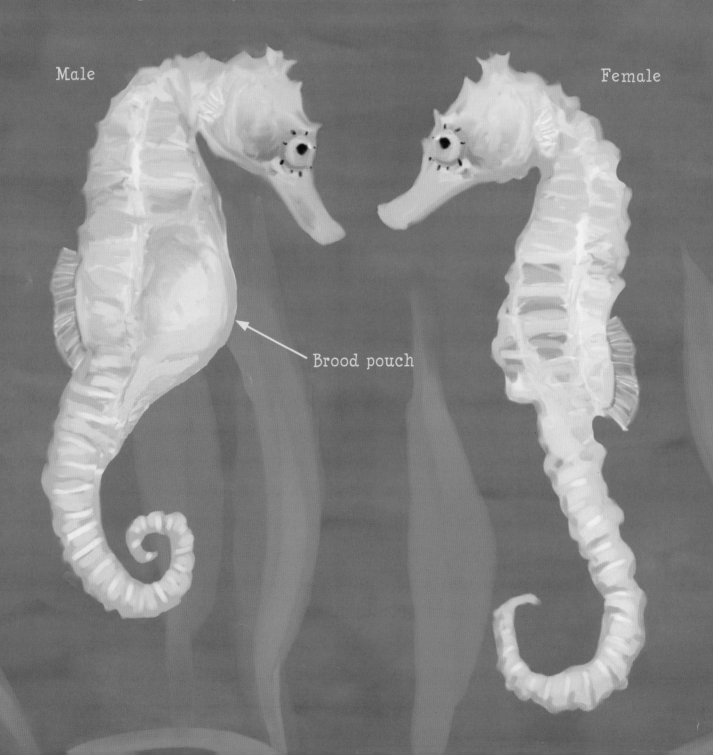

Male

Female

Brood pouch

8

The male sea horse washes his eggs and gives them oxygen. He also removes waste from the pouch. He makes the liquid inside the pouch more like salt water. When his babies are born, they will be used to salt water.

A few weeks later, my father's pouch opened. He latched his tail onto a blade of sea grass. He wriggled his body back and forth really hard.

Thirty of us were born. We were free to float and swim.

When a sea horse is born, it is only .32 inches
(8 millimeters) long. That is shorter than the length
of a staple! Once born, the tiny creature is on its
own, without any help from its parents.

My brothers, sisters, and I hooked tails. Soon we found a meadow of sea grass. Each one of us swam downward, grasping a blade.

I kept still and waited for food to float by. Then I pushed my body outward, face first. I sucked plankton and fish eggs into my snout. They were delicious!

A sea horse doesn't have teeth or a stomach. It sucks in food through its snout and passes the food through its digestive system.

Then I moved on. I swam until I saw a new bed of sea grass below me. I made my home there.

I'm hard to see because I change my color to blend into my surroundings. I hide from crabs and other fish. I wait for food to swim or drift by.

A sea horse lets small animals grow on its skin. The skin turns green, to match the sea grass.

I stay put most of the time because I can't swim fast. When I swim, I look like I'm standing up. I fan my dorsal fin, or the fin on my back, from side to side. I use my pectoral fins, or the fins on the sides of my head, to steer.

Pectoral fin

Dorsal fin

16

Because a sea horse can't move fast, it changes color to avoid fish who might want to eat it.

Even though I can't swim fast, I can stretch. When food passes by, I stretch my body and eat. My favorite meal is a tiny animal called a copepod.

A dwarf sea horse also eats fish eggs,
plankton, and drifting animals.

My life is slow, and I like it that way. I spend most of my time in the same spot—waiting, watching, eating, and breathing. I may live for only about a year. But in that time, I will find a partner and have babies, too.

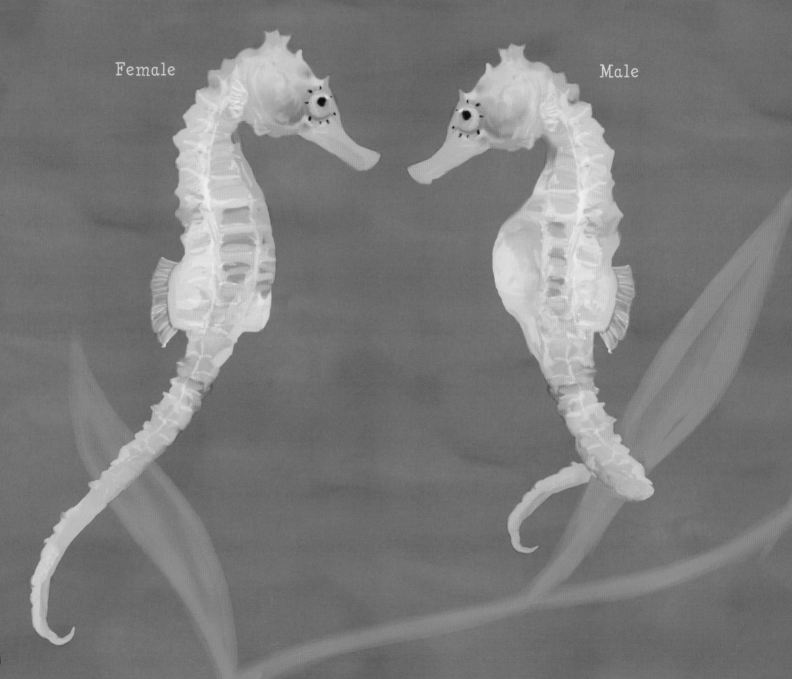

Female

Male

A sea horse uses gills to breathe. The gills are small and packed closely together. They take in oxygen from the water that flows over them.

Look Closely at a Dwarf Sea Horse

PECTORAL FINS keep the sea horse moving in the right direction.

TRUNK RINGS line the body. Not all sea horses have the same number of trunk rings.

The DORSAL FIN swings back and forth. It pushes the sea horse forward or backward.

A CORONET, or crown, is different on every dwarf sea horse.

Each of the two EYES can move in its own direction.

The SNOUT is shorter than those found on other kinds of sea horses.

GILLS are used to take in oxygen from the water.

BONY PLATES protect the body from predators.

A BROOD POUCH is found only on males. It holds the female's eggs after mating takes place.

The TAIL is used to grasp onto sea grass or coral.

Glossary

brood pouch—a hollow sack on an animal where eggs develop

copepod—a small freshwater or marine animal

dorsal fin—a fin located on the back

gills—part of a fish or tadpole that helps it breathe underwater

invertebrate—a creature without a backbone

oxygen—a gas in air or water that is important to all plants and animals

pectoral fins—a pair of fins found on each side of the head

plankton—small plants and animals that float in water

snout—the long front part of an animal's head that includes its nose, jaws, and mouth

Fun Facts

A True Name
A sea horse's scientific name, *Hippocampus*, is Greek for "horse sea monster."

Numbers
There are at least 34 known species of sea horses.

Size Means Everything
While it depends on the species, a sea horse can range in size from 1 inch (2.5 centimeters) to 12 inches (30.5 cm) long.

The Tiniest Sea Horse
Dwarf sea horses are often called "ponies." When they are fully-grown, they are only about 1 inch (2.5 cm) long.

The Life of a Sea Horse
Scientists don't have proof of exactly how long sea horses live. But they think that smaller ones live about one year. Larger ones might live about three to five years.

Watch Out!
Sea horses may become an endangered species because their habitat is slowly being destroyed. People also use them for traditional medicines to treat some diseases.

To Learn More

More Books to Read

Blackstone, Stella. *Secret Seahorse*. Cambridge, Mass.: Barefoot Books, 2005.

Butterworth, Chris. *Sea Horse: The Shyest Fish in the Sea*. Cambridge, Mass.: Candlewick Press, 2006.

Carle, Eric. *Mister Seahorse*. New York: Philomel Books, 2004.

James, Sylvia M. *Seahorses*. New York: Mondo, 2002.

On the Web

FactHound offers a safe, fun way to find Web sites related to topics in this book. All of the sites on FactHound have been researched by our staff.

1. Visit *www.facthound.com*
2. Type in this special code: 1404847286
3. Click the FETCH IT button.

Your trusty FactHound will fetch the best sites for you!

Index

Look for all of the books in the I Live in the Ocean series:

I Am a Dolphin:
The Life of a Bottlenose Dolphin

I Am a Fish:
The Life of a Clown Fish

I Am a Sea Horse:
The Life of a Dwarf Sea Horse

I Am a Sea Turtle:
The Life of a Green Sea Turtle

I Am a Seal:
The Life of an Elephant Seal

I Am a Shark:
The Life of a Hammerhead Shark

I Am a Whale:
The Life of a Humpback Whale

I Am an Octopus:
The Life of a Common Octopus